Deeper Walk

A Relevant Devotional Series

VOLUME 3

CONTEMPLATIONS FOR THE GOD-HUNGRY SOUL

BY THE EDITORS AND WRITERS OF RELEVANT MAGAZINE

Foreword by Winn Collier

Published by Relevant Books
A division of Relevant Media Group, Inc.

www.relevantbooks.com
www.relevantmediagroup.com

© 2004 by Relevant Media Group, Inc.

Design by Relevant Solutions
Cara Davis, Jeremy Kennedy
www.relevant-solutions.com

Relevant Books is a registered trademark of Relevant Media Group, Inc.,
and is registered in the U.S. Patent and Trademark Office.

Unless otherwise noted, Scripture quotations are taken from the HOLY BIBLE,
NEW INTERNATIONAL VERSION®. NIV®.
Copyright © 1973, 1978, 1984 by International Bible Society.
Used by permission of Zondervan Publishing House. All rights reserved.

Scripture quotations marked (NASB) are taken from NEW AMERICAN STANDARD BIBLE *
(NASB) © 1960, 1977, 1995 by the Lockman Foundation. Used by permission.

Scripture quotations marked (TLB) are taken from The Living Bible: Paraphrased by Kenneth Taylor.
Copyright © 1971 by Tyndale House Publishers.

Scripture quotations marked (MES) are taken from The Message by Eugene H. Peterson,
Copyright © 1993, 1994, 1995, 1996, 2000.
Used by permission of NavPress Publishing Group. All rights reserved.

Scripture quotations marked (NKJV) are taken from the New King James Version.
Copyright © 1979, 1980, 1982 by Thomas Nelson, Inc. Used by permission. All rights reserved.

Scripture quotations marked (AMP) are taken from The Amplified Bible. The Old Testament copyright
© 1965 by The Zondervan Corporation. The Amplified New Testament, copyright © 1954, 1958, 1987
by the Lockman Foundation. Used by permission.

Library of Congress Control Number: 2004093613
International Standard Book Number: 0-9746942-7-4

For information or bulk orders:
RELEVANT MEDIA GROUP, INC.
POST OFFICE BOX 951127
LAKE MARY, FL 32795
407-333-7152

04 05 06 07 9 8 7 6 5 4 3 2 1

Printed in the United States of America

Deeper Walk

A Relevant Devotional Series

VOLUME 3

CONTEMPLATIONS FOR THE
GOD-HUNGRY SOUL

BY THE EDITORS AND WRITERS OF RELEVANT MAGAZINE

Foreword by Winn Collier

❧CONTENTS❧

GOD OF CHANGE

CONTENTS

FOREWORD

The Gospels present numerous odd angles on the spiritual journey. In the words and ministry of Jesus, most religious assumptions—both of the first century and of today—are summarily overturned.

No Jesus-angle seems more odd, however, than His perplexing persistence in promoting the virtue of desperation. Whenever Christ speaks to those who are broken, bruised, or helpless—and know it—He calls them blessed, saying they are first in the Kingdom. On the other hand, whenever Christ encounters one who is smugly content, deluded by a misguided self-sufficiency, He firmly seeks to show them their scarred and destitute souls.

My own experience with Jesus connects with this pattern. In those seasons where I have felt adequate, adept at managing my life and maneuvering through the spiritual terrain stretched before me, my sense of self grows inflated. And sadly, my sense of God shrinks.

In these times, I live as if God is an addendum. I would never say as much, of course, but my actions speak for themselves. Far from needing God, I proceed as if He is a quaint and dainty presence. I am thankful to have Him near, and He is certainly welcome to stick around. But He isn't necessary.

Yet God is always necessary. He knows that only His words speak truth, only His mercy redeems hearts, only His death brings life. However, He will not force-feed us. He will not shove grace down our throat. We have to want it, to be hungry for it.

This is why Jesus sees desperation as virtuous. He wants us to crave what we don't have. He wants us to be hungry, ravenous, for Him.

Like the question Jesus posed to the lame beggar beside the pool of Bethesda, Jesus asks us, "Do we want to get well?" He asks us what it is we want, what it is we really desire.

The question to the beggar seems odd and the answer obvious. But apparently it wasn't quite so apparent. As the story is told, the beggar seems to waver, as if he might not know for sure what he desires. The life he has—hard as it is—is what he knows. It's safe. If he were to allow himself to really want something better, he might face the more severe ache of disappointment. The acute pain of shattered hopes is far more terrifying than the dull (yet constant) pain of never hoping at all.

Many of us find ourselves in a similar situation to the hope-refusing beggar. We would rather follow a tedious existence that is safe and mildly sufficient than to open ourselves to the possibility that there might be more to desire—because in the opening to more, there is the looming possibility of hopes unfulfilled.

We resonate with Anne Lamott's reflection on her years spent running from God. She recognized God was pursuing her, but she determined she was not "about to give up a life of shame and failure without a fight." Shame and failure, distressing as they are, just happen to be what we know. It's safer to settle than to let ourselves want for anything more.

So, we deny desire, and we ignore our hunger. But God keeps pointing out our nagging discontent, keeps reminding us what could be ours. He continues offering morsels of Himself. And if we will ever just take a taste, we will find ourselves famished for God.

Our deepest perceptions already tell us Who we crave. Our insatiable longings for the transcendent and the Divine are a constant whisper of our God-appetite. Even our sin is a steady murmur of our desires gone awry.

John Piper has reminded us that sin is what we do when we aren't feasting on the soul-nourishing pleasures of God. So, it would seem there are times when the proper anecdote to the allure of sin might not be another dose of rigorous, penitent self-denial but rather allowing ourselves, even encouraging ourselves, to be awakened to raw desire, to the famine of our soul. In these sensuous cravings, we will find the Spirit's invitation to come and dine.

But we will not come to God's banquet—we will not find satisfaction at His lavish, abundant table—until we really want it. Until we are hungry.

In the pages that follow, we hope to remind you of

your desires, to nurture in your soul a sense of the desperate. We hope that you will chew on what is offered and find that you are ravenous for God.

Eat and be filled.

Winn Collier, author and pastor

GOD

OF

HOPE

✣ LIVING IN ADVENT ✣
Winn Collier

Advent: the granddaddy of the Church's seasons. A four-week procession to Christmas, it is a richly textured and warmly symbolic stirring of hope and promise as the Church prepares for the celebration of the arrival of the Christ-child.

I love Advent, lighting the candles and hearing the stories. I chuckle as the kids participate with their large eyes and imaginations running wild. I cozy up to the smells and the sounds and the cheery-hearted sense that for at least a moment, all is right in the world.

Advent means "coming," and the power of Advent is that it reorients us to what is true: God. God entered the world. God stayed true to His promise. God came. He invaded a world writhing in despair and drowning in self-absorption. God came. And with Him came hope and redemption and a certainty that in the end, when He is finished, all that was lost in the fall will be restored.

But the tenuous nature of Advent is that in its reminder of God "coming," it also points to the future, to the reality that Christ is not finished, that all is not right in the world, that all lost in the fall is not yet restored.

And here we sit. In Advent. In between the coming and the coming again. We wait. We hope. We sin. We wonder. Sometimes, we forget.

Advent is fall and spring and summer. Advent is Easter and Christmas and every step between. When Advent is perceived "out of season," this is when we must remember all the more. So, contrary to Hallmark's opinion, Advent describes all of our days, days of waiting and hoping and wondering if it is all true, if it will all ever be true.

Yet, despite our doubts and our attempts to numb the waiting with smaller things and lesser hopes, there is something deep within our souls that will not let us forget, will not let us deny. We are people of the Advent, and we wait. We will wait until the end of time—if that is what is required—to see hope fulfilled and our God coming once again.

The moment of waiting and hoping, believing. And we live there in Advent every waking hour on this earth.

EVEN DEEPER
Isaiah 9, Revelation 21

PRAYER
Lord, deep down, I know there is a longing in me that will never be satisfied this side of heaven. I am waiting for Your return, Jesus. Help me to remember that You are coming. My hope is in my future with You.

WAIT, HOPE, TRUST
Tara Ringham

I've never heard the audible voice of God. I've heard stories about people hearing God audibly, but I've never experienced it myself. But there have been specific moments when His whisper inside of me is so strong, so clear, that I am completely overcome.

As I was driving my car one night, I had one of those "moments." God left me speechless with three simple words impressed in my mind: wait, hope, trust. That was all He spoke. But that was all He needed to say.

We all have obstacles in our lives that keep us from fully walking in the freedom that He died on the cross to give us—I like to think of them as mountains. In the midst of our storms, or even in the midst of our best days, we constantly ponder our purpose in life and dream of the greatness that lies ahead, whatever it may be. But we don't know how to obtain the faith that is required to move these mountains so that we may grab hold of the future we desire. Everything in our hearts wants to move them; yet sometimes, it seems easier to leave them there than change to the way things have always been. What if we fail?

As I sat in my car, I realized how much freedom could be found in those three simple words. But also I realized how I pick and choose which three I do. When I have time to sit at His feet, I wait. When I see the promise of something great on the horizon, I hope. When I see results to the countless prayers I have offered up, I trust.

I don't even view hope and trust as actions. They simply seem like nice "things" to possess in my Christian walk. But God is not calling us to pick and choose. He is calling us to fully embrace all three, for they cannot exist in their truest forms without one another.

We cannot wait on Him when we don't completely trust that He is in control and have a hope beyond doubt that His promises are true. We cannot have hope that His promises are for us unless we wait for Him to speak and reveal His will and trust that His plan is so much better than ours. We cannot fully trust in a God that we don't take the time to wait and grow in love with if our hope is not Him and Him alone.

As we do all three by the power of His grace, faith comes flooding in, and as Jesus revealed, we are able to move mountains with faith the mere size of a mustard seed. Maybe your mountain is an addiction. Maybe it's finally receiving complete acceptance or stepping out and doing what you know God's whisper has been speaking all along. Whatever the obstacle is, move it with the power He has given you, waiting, hoping, trusting.

EVEN DEEPER
Psalm 40, Isaiah 40:28-31, Proverbs 3:5-6

PRAYER
Lord, help me to learn to wait at Your feet and place all of my hope and trust in You. Increase my faith, that I may move this mountain and truly understand the greatness of your plans for me.

✒ THE VOICE OF EXPECTATION ✒
Stephanie Gehring

My friend loves doing things for people, as long as they don't expect it. Usually when people expect something from you, suddenly all they see is what you can do for them. They don't see you at all anymore.

Some expectations are stifling and oppressive. Others are scary, but full of hope. They say, "I know you're afraid to take the first step, but take it anyway. The next step will follow." Expectations can make us afraid to try anything new because it might not turn out—and it has to turn out.

Expectation can short-circuit life into depression, or it can send you flying off the edge of your world when you were sure you didn't have the courage to jump. The good type of expectation is a call to come because you need to grow, to create, because this is the place you are meant to be. It is an invitation: "Welcome, come in. You were expected." The bad type of expectation doesn't want you at all. It only wants what you produce, which is never good enough, and you must always do it all on your own.

That's how it works when evil speaks to us. It says that showing up is worth nothing; you're a failure from before the start. All your fears speak at once, as though they've already come true. The voice of evil is a self-fulfilling prophecy. Responsibility gets turned all on its head: The things we are really responsible for—showing up, being honest—are never even mentioned. Instead, evil loads us down with impossible demands: "Make miracles happen.

You call this creativity? You call this faith? Good grief. Maybe you really should give up. Spare the world more pointless junk. Who ever gave you the impression you could do this, anyway?"

But there, if we listen, is the weak spot in evil's argument. Art, great lives and achievements are never about small people who didn't have help. One-man success stories are slanted lies, and the truly successful are the first to point out: "Well, yes, I may have done the right thing; but you see none of it would ever have happened if it hadn't been for her. And him. And them."

Even the lonely things in life are never as lonely looking back as they seemed at the outset. God's good expectation calls you in poetry, saying, "Follow; it's okay sometimes not to know where you're going. We'll go together."

EVEN DEEPER
Isaiah 43:1-2

PRAYER
God, I don't want to act out of fear or the desire to please other people. I want to act out of obedience and boldness. Thank You for calling me to step out, expecting that You will work through me and guide me.

FROM REFLECTION TO REALITY
Erika Larson

1 Corinthians 13, which opens with, "Love is patient, love is kind," is a well-known passage of Scripture for those who have grown up in church. I've heard this passage used at Christian weddings umpteen times. It paints an inspiring picture of love that is totally selfless, looking to others' best interests and totally free from fear.

It's appropriate that these verses show up at weddings, as marriage is the closest picture of the love relationship Jesus wants to have with the Church. Marriage is the fullest and most intimate expression of real love. As Christ pursues us, so the groom pursued his bride, eventually humbling himself to lower to one knee and offer a costly gift—the ring—which essentially buys her, claims her as his. As she accepts his gift, she says "yes" to a life with him, takes his name, and pursues him back, and they enter into a shared life of service and submission to one another. They live out the description of love found in 1 Corinthians.

But that's not all. After the vows are said and the bouquet and garter are tossed, the new married couple goes off to finally know each other as deeply as anyone can be known in a physical sense. The act of making love, which solidifies the couple's oneness, represents a knowing that is deep and beautiful and mysterious.

The deepest desire of the human soul is to be known. To be understood. To be explored and found desirable. This mutual knowing is the ultimate closeness. But as the years of marriage pass, both partners realize that though they know each other deeply, though they know more about each other than anyone else, there's still more to learn, more to probe. As known as they are, they are not fully known. In verse 12 of 1 Corinthians, Paul says, "Now we see but a poor reflection as in a mirror; then we shall see face to face. Now I know in part; then I shall know fully, even as I am fully known."

Marriage, as well as other forms of intimate earthly love, is just a poor reflection of the love—the full knowing—we look forward to. As we can't fully know our spouse or other loved ones, we can't fully know Jesus, but we are told that He knows us fully, and someday we'll know Him. Free from the insecurities, wounds, and flawed ideas that hold us back now, free from any of the selfishness that seems so impossible to escape here in this world, we'll be able to fully give and receive love. All the best examples you've ever experienced of intimate love and knowing all put together are but a poor reflection, like a dusty, cracked mirror in an attic. We've got the real thing coming.

EVEN DEEPER
1 Corinthians 13, Romans 8:35-39, Isaiah 54:5

PRAYER
Jesus, I am excited to be face to face with You. It's hard to even fathom. Thank You for giving us pictures on earth of Your love for us. Thank You that You fully know me, and that someday I'll fully know You.

❧A BEGGING FAITH☙
Andrew Albers

I pass by the third homeless person on Mass Avenue and do not stop to give him any change. A few lonely coins rattle around the bottom of his grimy Big Gulp cup as I cruise to the subway stop. How does my faith guide me in this moment? If the kingdom of God is seen in the "least" among us, what have I just missed? What have I just refused to see as I passed by this stranger asking for spare change?

What's the meaning of faith when we don't even recognize the kingdom of God when it stretches its very hand out to us? Hebrews 11:1 tells us, "faith is being … certain of what we do not see."

How can I be "faithful" in that sense when I can't even acknowledge when God is visibly, physically reaching out to me on the street corner?

2 Corinthians 4:17-18 reminds us, "Our light and momentary troubles are achieving for us an eternal glory that far outweighs them all. So we fix our eyes not on what is seen, but on what is unseen. For what is seen is temporary, but what is unseen is eternal."

Is this passage meant to give hope to the homeless man in Harvard Square? Or is it a sentence of condemnation for me?

If you want to get biblical about it, the homeless man and I are the same person. We are all broken, all beggars, without hierarchy. Whether for spare change, for food, for mercy, for forgiveness—we are all begging, desperate and in need. We all must reveal our desperation and open ourselves to receiving grace. And we are all called to be Christ's hands in those moments—stopping, bending down and serving.

If Christ is true, if the Gospel is true, it would seem that seeing Christ in the beggar as well as seeing the beggar in me reflects the reality of what Paul tells the Corinthians is both "eternal" and "unseen."

As we embrace, by faith, the reality of God that stands (or sits or begs) in front of us, we are in that moment living for another world, a truer world. In that moment, we are echoing our belief that the pleasure of God's reality, what Paul calls "eternal glory," is more authentic than what is "seen"—the world's illusions and delusions grabbing for our allegiance.

Perhaps being faithful is believing and living like there is truly no difference between any of us.

EVEN DEEPER
Matthew 25:31-46, 2 Corinthians 4, Hebrews 11

PRAYER
Lord, I confess to You that I am just as weak and broken as those who I perceive as being needy. I thankfully receive Your grace. Help me to live for "eternal glory" by serving those around me.

❧ THE RISK OF HOPE ❧
Winn Collier

A cynic is one who has been wounded by hope, who
has, as Solomon put it, had "hope deferred." A deferred
hope is to have a promise go unfulfilled or dreams dis-
sipate. A deferred hope is to have our passions yield more
sorrow than joy. The wisdom writer said, "Hope deferred
makes the heart sick" (Proverbs 13:12). Wisdom indeed.

A sick heart is a heart that has been trampled on,
bruised, and ignored. It is a heart that has stared down
the shadowy abyss of loss and shame, and has been
unable to see anything beyond it. A sick heart has caved
in to the unrelenting pressure of a hope postponed far
too long.

Hope does not, as some suggest, "spring eternal." A
fully redeemed hope would offer an unending supply
of optimistic anticipation, but unfortunately, nothing
in this tragic world is fully redeemed. So, at moments,
ecstatic joys pierce our hearts, and hope flourishes. In
other moments, distressing realities overcome us, and
hope languishes. This dichotomy we live—between a
flourishing and a languishing hope—is normal, part
of the routine of the human condition. Some simply
refer to it as life. Uncomfortable as it is, it does not
debilitate. It does not paralyze. We don't look forward to
this swinging pendulum, but we expect it. And in each
stormy episode, we find ourselves looking up for the next
hopeful ray to break through our overcast hearts.

The tragedy is not in these customary dim days where
hope is briefly muffled. The tragedy is when we sur-

render our hearts to these murky shadows, and in doing so, hope is ultimately silenced. For some of us, we have been disappointed one time too many. The pain to hope has grown too difficult, and our sick hearts have believed a fatal lie: The risk of hoping is more costly than the benign shelter found in never hoping at all.

When we take that misguided turn, we cede passion, desire and all that offers us life. We become cynics in order to stymie hope before it can ever take root, before it can ever disappoint. We nurture the belief that what we are is all we ever will be, and we settle in for a safe, shallow and utterly empty existence. We become like Snoopy. "Yesterday I was a dog. Today I'm a dog. Tomorrow I'll probably still be a dog. Sigh! There's so little hope for advancement."

Solomon concludes his proverb with a challenge to the cynic: "but desire fulfilled is a tree of life." The antidote to the sick heart of disappointed hopes is to give way to desire, to make room for it ... to hope for it. To hope for God.

It's dangerous. The disappointment will mount, and it will be costly. But it is the only way to life, to truly live.

EVEN DEEPER
Proverbs 13:12, Matthew 4:1-11

PRAYER
Lord, I will take the risk to hope. I will risk disappointment. Make me fully alive in You.

❦ PERFECT WORLD ❦

Doug Floyd

He's in the middle of a thriving culture, the middle of an extensive family and the middle of his father's house. He's in the middle of it all, and he leaves—never to return. Abraham chooses exile. Like a fugitive, he leaves the safety and identity of the past behind and follows a call into the middle of nothing and nowhere, searching for the place that is beyond all.

Searching, always searching, Abraham keeps searching for the perfect place. Nothing and nowhere else will do. The only place his weary limbs can rest is in that perfect place.

In the middle of his search, Isaac appears like a kiss from heaven, bringing a smile to Abraham's desert-cracked face. Yet once again, in the middle of it all, Abraham is told to go forth. Before, he left his past behind. Now, he must leave his future behind. On the sacred mountain, Abraham says goodbye to his inheritance and offers Isaac to God. In the middle of the sacrifice, an angel stops him and offers a ram instead. Isaac lives, yet Abraham has already left.

He is searching, looking for his inheritance: the city of God. From time to time, he sees a faint glimpse of a glory that surpasses all glory. And this glory is enough to keep the search alive.

So often, we reject pilgrimage and instead look for heaven on earth. We have fewer dangers and enjoy more freedoms and luxuries than any people throughout history, and somehow, we think we deserve more.

So we look for perfect marriages, perfect jobs, perfect houses, perfect friendships, perfect vacations and perfect churches. Yet none of these exist. We are not in heaven. Rather, we've been called to pilgrimage.

In the middle of it all, we are invited to leave. In the middle of our high paying jobs, in the middle of our comfortable homes, in the middle of our fractured families, we're called to pilgrimage. We're called to a city whose author and founder is God.

As exiles on this earth, we wander and wonder, receiving every breath as a gift from our Father in heaven. He is leading us through the land of letting go so that we might rest in the land of warm embrace.

Instead of worrying about why we don't have the fastest car or the biggest house or the perfect life, let us welcome the invitation to journey and celebrate each moment on the way to our Father's house.

EVEN DEEPER
Hebrews 11:13-16, Psalm 84:5-7, Genesis 22

PRAYER
Father, help me to let go of the "heaven on earth" I try to make for myself. I want to know in my heart of hearts that my true home is not this world, but it is with You in heaven. As I journey through this life, keep me thankful and faithful.

✍ **BETTER THAN A FAIRYTALE** ✎
Stephanie Gehring

The idea of heaven used to scare me. Mostly, I was afraid of the boredom—imagine doing the same thing, forever. No end. I've heard that perfection excludes boredom—but I've also heard that imperfections make life interesting.

As Christians, we are called to imagine the unimaginable. I misunderstand perfection if I believe that imperfections are what provide life its spice. This assertion might be true now, but here's the thing: We're not in heaven. When we fall down here, our knees get bloody and our shins get scuffed. We are forced to face pain. When we lose something here, we grasp and cling to what we still have. We grow acutely aware of want and regret. These are moments with God. Here, now, we must have our lives knocked out of our hands if we're ever to hold anything worth keeping.

But imagine: It is not the place that matters; it is you. Imagine you're different; imagine you don't have to lose to know. Imagine you don't have to fall to let yourself be held. Imagine you do not cling to power like a despot; imagine you give it away without fear. You're connected to a current so strong, you know it will carry you. For the first time, you trust freely.

You're at the gates, and the light on your face is alive. Already it knows you, and for a split second you dare to forget who you are; the beauty is enough. Then your name returns to you, and it has changed. Now you know what it means.

If we don't really believe in heaven—so deeply that it captures our hopes and our dreams—then something is terribly wrong. Our foundation has slipped. Heaven teaches us how to live in our world. If we lose our vision of heaven, we lose our vision for today.

Welcome to mystery. You have entered the land where dreamers live, the saints and poets Thornton Wilder talked about in *Our Town*, the only ones who might know life while they lived it—every moment.

Live is the key word; it is the reason heaven matters. Heaven is high-voltage life. Heaven is beauty enough to get drunk on. Heaven is huge. You will never arrive at its end; you will never tire of the journey, because it's a journey into the pulsing heart of God. Fear has no home there.

Heaven is not a myth. And perfection is not boring.

EVEN DEEPER
1 Corinthians 12, 2 Corinthians 5:4, Matthew 6:20, Revelation 5:13

PRAYER
Lord, give me a vision of heaven that is so grand that I can't help but be filled with anticipation. Thank You that it is reality, that it is coming, that it is beauty itself. I know so little about heaven. I commit to understanding it better.

HOPE REMAINS
Stephanie Gehring

As soul-sicknesses go, hopelessness is among the most deadly. When Paul said faith, hope, and love are the three things that remain, this is part of what he meant: Losing any one of them will cripple you, rob you of something essential; without them, real life is not possible.

Hopelessness is an egalitarian disease. You do not have to be old to catch it. Money will not save you from it; neither will beauty. You can catch it anywhere; the air is full of it. It feeds you this lie: that you know how the story will end, your story, and that it is not an end worth living for. There is no hope, not for your life.

Hope is not optimism. Living in hope does not mean having a good feeling about tomorrow. Neither is hope knowledge in an intellectual sense—you do not hope 2 and 2 equal 4. The certainty of elementary math is not the certainty of hope.

Hope is not mental acrobatics or positive thinking. It is what happens inside you when God's Spirit comes and carries you past death and into life. Hope means death can break your heart, but it can't kill you anymore. It can't win. The war to end all wars has been fought. It has been won, past tense, and now history has no choice: The end will be good, no matter what.

In an essay on storytelling, J.R.R. Tolkien makes the claim that all true stories must end in eucatastrophe, which is more than your run-of-the-mill happy ending— it is a clashing, surging chaos like a natural disaster, like a catastrophe, except that instead of terror and destruction, it brings about life. Stories can end in despair, but then they are only telling part of the real story; they are not going all the way to the end. Eucatastrophe is the truth, he says, because it has happened. In Christ's living and His dying, there was catastrophe—but in His rising from the grave, catastrophe was flipped on its head; nothing will ever be the same. And, as Paul said, "hope remains."

We could not hope without Christ's life and without His Spirit in us, making us certain of this thing we have not seen. Some call it glory, meaning something like, "essential, absolute life." We will not see it here except in glimpses, but it has been promised, forever, with shattering finality.

EVEN DEEPER
Colossians 1:24-27, Hebrews 11

PRAYER
Jesus, thank You that You have made the end good. May I live and walk in that hope, and bring it to the hopeless.

THE LIFE AND DEATH OF AN EXPECTATION
Allison Foley

Picture a shape of some sort, perhaps a kind of blob, and let that represent an expectation at its conception. Even before anything happens, we know what we want to see in that expectation for it to be fulfilled and complete. You have an expectation of what healing is going to look like in your life, and it includes certain components. When one of those components actually comes to pass, it takes its place in the expectation without a second thought, as if it's expected to be there. Thus there's really no need to acknowledge it, and it becomes an item on a checklist.

But the problem is that eventually, huge chunks of the expectation will not be fulfilled. God might let us have our way for a little while and think that we're in control, but He will show us that we don't have absolute power to create our reality. But since the fulfilled chunks of the expectation don't count—remember, they were all but dismissed when they occurred—all we see left is the part left unfinished, and we label ourselves "failures," "bad Christians," and a host of other destructive names. Rather than being motivated to do better next time, we get mad at ourselves, at God, and at people who were part of the plan in our expectations (whom, by the way, we can't control). No, this type of kick in the pants is not what's going to boost you into spiritual high gear. Not to mention that you'll be a really difficult person to be around because these unfulfilled expectations will affect everyone with whom you come into contact. The point here is that expectations have a huge impact on how we perceive our experiences. It makes no difference that they're "just in your head," if in fact they shape your life the way they do.

Don't give up on dreaming big and believing for God to do amazing things in your life. That's not the problem because the desire within us to live a miraculous and relationally rich life is wonderful. But be aware of your attitude toward the events that play into your expectations. Are you grateful for each fulfillment ... truly grateful? Do you place a lot of your hopes for the next event in what has already happened? Do you still know that God is working His own plan out and that He doesn't need your help? Live for the moment, be contemplatively thankful, and know that He is God.

EVEN DEEPER
James 4:15, Proverbs 19:21

PRAYER
Lord, forgive me for always telling You what to do. You know best. Thank You for these present circumstances—the joys and the frustrations.

A BACKWARDS WORLD
Winn Collier

Christ was constantly saying things that were entirely out of order. If you want to keep living, abandon your life. If someone slaps you across the face, offer them your other cheek. If you want to be truly rich, give everything away.

None of Christ's teachings were more out of order, more backwards, than the Beatitudes, the rapid-shock introduction to His infamous Sermon on the Mount. Massive crowds had gathered around Jesus, and He had spent hours touching and healing the lepers' puss-filled sores and the crusted, scabby eyes of those who had never seen a sunset or the hands of those dropping a few coins in their cup. He had spent His day with the rejects, the outcasts.

Most of the religious power-holders recoiled with disgust as Jesus embraced the unclean in their filth. Some endured His actions, assuming they were patronizing acts of piety.

Whatever disdain they harbored, it provided no opportunity to prepare them for the subversive words Christ would soon speak: Blessed are the poor in spirit, for theirs is the kingdom of heaven.

And as if He hadn't said enough, He didn't stop there. The Beatitudes continue with Jesus' announcement that it is not only the poor, but also the emotional wrecks, the weak and the routinely dismissed who are truly blessed. The helpless who are constantly stepped on and abused receive all the luxuries of the kingdom of God.

Jesus lives in one backwards world.

But, if we are honest, this is good news. This is Gospel. We are all poor in spirit. We are all weak and helpless. And if we embrace it, we find ourselves knee-deep in redemption, smothered in hope and freedom. Blessed.

Christ's words speak life to us. Blessed are you who have flunked out, boozed out, doped out. Blessed are you whose bodies are wracked with AIDS, who have been fired from your job, whose marriages are falling apart. Blessed are all of you who are on the brink of despair. Blessed are all of you.

One crazy, backwards world. So backwards it would require a Savior, a cross and an empty tomb.

Fredrick Buechner highlighted the lunacy: "If the world is sane, then Jesus is mad as a hatter and the Last Supper is the Mad Tea Party. In terms of the world's sanity, Jesus is as crazy as a coot, and anybody who thinks he can follow Him without being a little crazy too is laboring less under the cross than under a delusion."

One crazy, backwards world.

EVEN DEEPER
Matthew 5-7, Luke 6

PRAYER
Jesus, please help me to think the way You think. Give me Your eyes when I look at the world. Thank You that in my brokenness, You prove Your power of redemption. My hope is not in myself; it's in You.

⚘ HOLDING LIGHT ⚘
Stephanie Gehring

The world is gray again. There seems to be no point in loving, in believing, in giving—not when everything you touch dies anyhow. And doesn't it? That's how the world works. Things don't stay beautiful, people don't stay alive. Call it divorce, call it cancer, call it time; it is no lie to say you're dying today. So am I. So is everything.

And how could you hope? There would have to be someone to trust whose word speaks stronger than what seems so real. And then you would have to believe. Somehow you would have to hold light, to reflect something bright even when you're surrounded by gray. You'd need to be exchanged on the inside, be made of different stuff. Then you wouldn't change colors with the world. Things could go from gray to black without turning you dark—if you were made of something new.

God speaks the words that last; may we dare to trust and hear. Let us give ourselves to God, in tiny bits at first, let us find the pieces are held safe. We will dare to give bigger pieces eventually, and even bigger, until we'll throw ourselves off anything as long as the one we trust is there calling.

Let us hear. Let us begin to stay honest when we feel like lying, let us not pretend to have heard what we wanted rather than what was said. We must learn not to flee from the truth anymore. We must learn to hold still. Even though holding still with the truth can take more trust than leaping off a cliff.

But if you trust God enough to hold still with the truth (just a little bit at a time), your insides will—slowly—be changed into the kind of stuff that holds light. Hope is not about the color of your world. It's about the color of what lasts, about the light that comes through sometimes. It is the reason, C.S. Lewis said, that artists paint: because they catch glimpses of heaven. Hope is about remembering the light you've seen and about looking ahead to the light you can't see yet.

Hope is being fully alive. If you hope you will be a bright tear in the fabric of this world; you will be a place where people can see through, can be changed.

EVEN DEEPER
1 Corinthians 13:10

PRAYER
God, in this moment, I'm quiet, thinking back to the times You've given me glimpses of the better world that's coming. I'm letting my imagination take me to what that better world might be like. Thank You that there is hope.

❧ EXTRAVAGANT REALITY ❧
Leslie Davies

"God is that extravagant."

It was a simple yet remarkable observation from my friend about a television show we had just watched, *Extreme Makeover: Home Edition*. In this segment, the design team remodeled the entire home of a large family in which both parents had recently died. When the children were brought in to see the changes, they burst into a combination of joyful shrieks and sobs. They were stunned by the utter extravagance of such a gift.

In my life, when I'm stunned by God's extravagance, I consider what the "long tomorrow," as A.W. Tozer labeled eternity, will be like. What stunning things does God have in store for those who believe? What will we do forever? In his book *Money, Possessions & Eternity*, Randy Alcorn said, "We were made for a person and a place. Jesus is the person. Heaven is the place."

The Bible is replete with images and suggestions of heaven's reality. We know that eternal life will be centered on serving and worshiping God. We'll feel perfectly at home. We'll meet and converse with other beings in heaven. We'll rest and feast, and at the same time, we'll also lead and make important decisions. Without the limitations of sin and death, we'll be fully creative and joyful as we reign with God.

In the book of Jeremiah, we read that, "I, the Lord, search the heart, I test the mind, even to give to every man according to his ways, according to the fruit of his doings." We have received salvation as a *free gift*; beyond that, His Spirit moves us to do the good works for which we were created—and for which we will be rewarded. The biblical authors mention works such as putting others' needs ahead of our own, suffering for His sake, showing compassion to the needy, treating enemies kindly and giving generously. These works spread the Gospel message. We accomplish them by using what He gives us daily—time and energy, money and possessions. Some rewards come in this life; the greater ones will come in heaven.

As Christians, we trust in a God we can't yet see and a reality still to come. Heaven will be a remarkable existence, filled with extravagance beyond our imagination. Evangelist D.L. Moody commented appropriately, "Soon you will read in the newspaper that I am dead. Don't believe it for a moment. I will be more alive than ever before."

EVEN DEEPER
Deuteronomy 28:1-14, Revelation 21 & 22

PRAYER
My God and King, sometimes I see bits of glory here in this life, and it reminds me that You have a stunning surprise waiting for me. Help me then to live selflessly, generously with what You give me. My hope is in You.

৵DRAWING FROM THE WELL৶
Kate Bryan

I've been reading about different personality types in a book called *Discovering the Enneagram* by Richard Rohr and Andreas Ebert (Crossroad/Herder & Herder). It's the first stab at defining personalities that has ever made any sense to me.

The category I fall into mentions living out of a deep sense of loss and shame. Shame. This word reverberates inside of me every time I hear it. It's a part of me. It was at some point kneaded into the makeup of my being, and there it has remained.

I have been thinking about the woman at the well lately. About the way that Jesus chose that place to essentially (metaphorically) propose, and how that woman was to be His bride. He ripped through eternity and the heavens and through a womb, and He didn't stop until He sat there on the side of that well. He ripped into the heart of a nobody, a woman broken and despised, shameful, and said, "I choose you." She came with her bucket to fill and left it there with Him. I can imagine it lying on its side next to Jesus' feet, dropped and forgotten in the ecstasy of being known by God.

The moments of panic will come and go when my value is assigned by the world's standards. There will be times when I feel alone and defenseless against its judgment. But this is what is REAL: Jesus told the woman at the well that the time has come when the true worshipers will worship in spirit and in truth.

Essentially, He was saying: "I am it. The spirit world is

more real than the ground you stand on. Let my voice be the well from which you draw, and the voice to which all other voices are compared."

EVEN DEEPER
John 4:1-42, Joel 2:27, Ezekiel 16:8

PRAYER
Jesus, thank You for taking away my shame and choosing me. Each day, remind me that I have value in You. May Your voice be the clearest in my head.

ETERNITY—RIGHT UNDER YOUR NOSE
Allison Foley

If you listen closely, you'll frequently hear people say something like, "There's gotta be a better way," "That's just not right," and "This isn't the way it's supposed to be." Even from a young age, children cry: "It's not fair!" They're right. It's not fair. This isn't the way it's supposed to be. Things in this life don't fit.

C.S. Lewis, in the book *A Severe Mercy* by Sheldon Vanauken (Hodder and Stoughton), used the concept of time to say we've been made for something greater. To paraphrase, if we were fish, we would not complain about living in water; it would be we were designed for. But living as humans in time, we're never quite satisfied with how it all goes: We feel cheated by the brevity of time, while frustrated with time that seems to drag on. We are surprised by the abruptness of death in a young one, and the delay of death in an elderly or terminal loved one who is suffering. And yet it's not the fault of time—time is constant! Lewis, then, says we feel out of place in time because we were made for a timeless existence.

Similarly, we have ideals about justice and what is good. Whether we are rallying for that justice to be accomplished through peace or through warfare, we want to fix what is not right and bring ultimate justice to that which is unjust. We cannot seem to agree as a global community on what that really looks like, and yet we all desire it. Our relativistic society says that everyone's good is good, but how can so many conflicting notions of that good really be in harmony?

King Solomon said, "God has placed eternity in the hearts of men." The Amplified Bible continues, "[which is] a divine, implanted sense of a purpose working through the ages which nothing under the sun but God alone can satisfy." We will never see an agreement about how to effect justice or a definitive list on right and wrong with which the whole world agrees. Even Christians are divided on issues where opinions are formed by the Bible and by the tradition of the Church. You were made for something greater. We have these greater ideals set in our hearts—eternity set in our hearts—because God created us for more than this. Rather than being a frustration, it can be a great comfort when the world and this life disappoint. Where do you connect most with the eternity that God has put in your heart? What does a life look like when one lives with eternity in mind? Take comfort in eternity.

EVEN DEEPER
Ecclesiastes 3:11a, 2 Corinthians 4:17-18

PRAYER
God, life on this earth is confusing and often painful. I believe there is a better way. Help me to find comfort in and connect with the coming reality.

❦ HOPE NOW ❧
Eric Hurtgen

Help is finally available. At least that must have been
what the throng of city folks were thinking as they fol-
lowed Jesus out of town, up into the hills. Hadn't He
just healed their friends and family members of lifelong
pain, disabling disease, even paralysis? This was the kind
of help the crowds understood. This aid for the ailing
was not just the distant promise of eternal bliss or the
propaganda of an idealist revolutionary; this help was
much nearer, located in the tangible now rather than the
unknown tomorrow. It took no clever ad campaigns to
mobilize the multitudes. Jesus' following was a natural
response to the promise of healing and wholeness.

Certainly, the crowds hung on Jesus' every word. His
credentials were draped across the shoulders of all those
who had been sick and were now well. The words He
spoke were charged with electricity, surprising and super-
naturally real. As He taught the multitudes from the
natural pulpit of the mountainside, He elaborated on
the hope of generations. The throng must have listened
in rapt attention as He detailed the finer points of a new
kind of life, a kind of life that emerged from a reality He
knew so well.

As Jesus taught, He gave a look at a life lived in tan-
dem with God, a life bristling with an otherworldly
energy. Hope could now be found on the horizon, right
around the bend, or right here! Jesus offered His students
a chance to join God in His exploits every day, to hold
fresh hope out to the world. This offer of supernatural

interaction was deeply imbedded in the prayer Jesus suggested on the mountainside:

Our Father in heaven, your name is holy. Let your kingdom come, let your will be done on earth like it is in heaven. Give us what we need for today. Forgive us our debts and we'll forgive those in debt to us. And don't lead us into places of temptation, but get us out of evil.

Jesus was not holding out the idealism of some sweet by and by, merely passing out some religious opiate for the masses; Jesus was teaching the crowds to ask God to be involved with them today. And by today, He meant right now. Let God's kingdom come now. Give us sustenance today, not at some undisclosed time in the future.

This was no twentieth-century style prosperity gospel; Jesus would later explain that troubles would surely come, but this was the proclamation of God come to earth. And He had come to earth with a reckless love that would not wait for "the other side of eternity" to bless His people, He wanted to give them a reality to place their hope in. He was opening up the doors of His kingdom, calling all who would listen. And His kingdom, His reality, His help is still available for all those who would hear His voice and would answer. Even now.

EVEN DEEPER
Matthew 6:9-13, Colossians 1

PRAYER
God, thank You that hope isn't only for the future—it is for today.

❧ LOOKING UP ❧
Stephanie Gehring

Righteousness—isn't that what some really loud preachers always talk about? And the people who give you guilt trips because you don't study the Bible at least fifteen hours per day?

To Jesus, righteousness is not stiff. It is not a weight to crush you; it is not a rule to follow. It is more like an elemental gladness: the giddy gladness from which life sprang in the beginning of all things. Righteousness, Jesus says, is so good that if you so much as long for it, you should be counted among the luckiest of people: for God will fill you.

Righteousness is being able to want yes, to say yes, and then to do yes. Righteousness is being able to walk without falling on the people you love and hurting them. It is being able to hold something precious safely, without dropping it to shatter on the ground. Righteousness is the song that makes the world alive; it is a caterpillar's knowing to wrap itself in silk, the silk's turning hard, and the caterpillar's metamorphosis, the glory of flight on new wings.

Righteousness is something entirely different from trying to do the right thing. Righteousness is the way we live when we've been made new inside, when we've been filled. This is essential. I can try to do the right thing. I should try to do the right thing. But real righteousness is about who I am. And I can no more make myself be different, in my invisible self, than I can suddenly choose, in my body, not to be made of 97 percent water. It's not possible. I could stop drinking anything, and in less than a week, when I'm dead, I might have reduced my water percentage to 90 percent. I am what I am; if I am to be something else, the change must happen through power beyond mine.

We're not talking about hard work here; we're talking about miracle. That's where longing comes in, hungering and thirsting: We cannot make this thing happen. We cannot cause, or force, or speed up our becoming right; we cannot lessen the degree of our wrongness. But we can look up. We can see what is good, and though we may see no good in ourselves, we can let ourselves cry out with wanting, with hunger, to be what we are not.

It is a wonderful promise Jesus makes here—that in just looking up, fixing our eyes on what is good, admitting the ache of our inadequacy, we become blessed ones. God knows what you are made of, Jesus seems to be saying. That is why God asks you only for your emptiness: It is all you have to give.

And it is enough.

EVEN DEEPER
2 Corinthians 5:16-21, Matthew 5:6

PRAYER
Father, make me new inside. Place a craving for righteousness in my heart. Transform me. Thank You that because of Your power and grace, I am blessed and holy.

❦ WELCOME TO THE BANQUET ❧
Winn Collier

If you haven't seen the movie *Antwone Fisher*, slowly close this book and go immediately to your neighborhood video store. G.K. Chesterton said every good story is a retelling of the Gospel. Antwone Fisher offers the Gospel in IMAX. In many ways, Antwone's story could be told a thousand times over: A baby grows up an abused orphan through the flawed social services system. Forced to come to terms with the destructive anger seething just under the surface, Antwone embarks on a redemptive journey to find his roots and his family. He sets out to find forgiveness: both to give and to receive. The story is plainly told, straightforward and almost methodical. The story's climax comes after Antwone finds his mom, a disappointing encounter where he tells her who he has become as a man while she sits silent, eyes glued to the floor in shame.

He returns to the home of his aunt (the sister of his dead father who he never knew) and opens the door, surprised to find a mob of people. Children and couples and cousins and uncles and family friends all smother him with hugs and beaming smiles. He is led to a grand feast. The scene is a party. For the first time in his life, he is being adored; he belongs.

As the clamor quiets, an elderly woman sitting behind the table motions for him. With slow, deliberate moves, she caresses his face. A tear runs down her cheek, and with a raspy voice that seems as if it were mustering all the strength it possessed, she whispers the most redemp-

tive word he has ever heard: "Welcome."

Welcome to the life of a man who had never been truly welcomed anywhere. Welcome to a feast in his honor when no one had ever shown delight in him before. Welcome to a home, a people. Welcome.

"Welcome" is the core of the Gospel.

Welcome if you are scarred by sin. Welcome if you have never heard anyone call out your name with shee pleasure. Welcome if notions of acceptance and love h only mocked you. Welcome if you have abandoned ho that you could ever find a home.

This is God's invitation: a hearty welcome to the-banquet, where joy, laughter and a deep embracing are yours. The prophetic invitation which peered ahead to cross is this: "The Lord Almighty will prepare a feast o rich food for all peoples, a banquet of aged wine—the best of meats and the finest of wines."

Welcome to the banquet.

EVEN DEEPER
Isaiah 25, Exodus 2, Acts 28, Revelation 19:6-9

PRAYER
Lord, thank You for making a place for me at Your wedding banquet table. Help me to live my life in light of that coming reality and to seek my sense of belonging and acceptance in You first.

GOD
OF
CHANGE

✒ SUBVERSIVE TRANSFORMATION ✑
Winn Collier

Crete was a thoroughly pagan society, a resort destination for aristocrats and financial tycoons. Drowning in greed and self-absorption, this small city-island off the coast of Italy was consumed with high stakes and fast times. If you weren't a power-grabber, Crete was not your kind of town.

The Gospel held no sway here, and Paul, who always seemed to draw a bull's-eye on the unlikeliest of destinations, decided it was time for Christ's message to make its mark. And he thought Titus was just the guy to lead the operation. Titus' task was simple, singular: ignite a movement that will transform the hearts, minds, and culture of this pagan people. It was no small order. Titus must have felt a bit overwhelmed.

Paul left a few instructions, directives Titus was to pass on to those he would influence. What do you imagine Titus thought as he read the words: Have self-control. Don't get drunk. Be disciplined. Love your family. Have integrity. Did I already mention not to get drunk?

Did Paul not get that Cretans only understood two things: muscle and cash? Wouldn't Titus need to organize a political alliance to influence public opinion, or raise capital to provide the economic means to play hardball the way the Cretans were used to seeing it done?

Apparently not. His words were as clear as they were simple. Love well. Have good character. Be honest at your job.

Perhaps Paul knew God's transforming work happens in small, quiet, and subversive ways. Perhaps Paul knew that if the Church allowed the systems of this world to pull us onto their turf, using power and control as our means of engagement, we would end up with much of what the modern Church has now become.

We are fat with resources, organized to efficiency and comfortably self-sufficient. Yet, with all this in our supposed favor, we are weak in Spirit, often removed from the very people God would have us impact, and rarely do we experience genuine, God-breathed transformation.

Crete sounds little different from our culture. Perhaps we should return to Titus and Paul's straightforward words. What if we radically loved and truly forgave? What if integrity defined us, character shaped us, and there was never any question of where our loyalties lie?

What if, rather than forcing our way in, we gave ourselves away? What if we made smaller demands and had quieter voices? What if we had larger hearts consumed with a more radical grace?

We might see transformation … the subversive type.

EVEN DEEPER
Titus 2

PRAYER
God, I truly desire to live a transformed life, and I feel far from that. Change me in small ways—in everyday ways. May I show love and integrity at work and in my daily interactions with people.

THE STRUGGLE TO LOVE
Derek Webb

I love someone who is gay. She knows me well, knows I don't condone the gay lifestyle because of my beliefs. So, what do I do with this situation? Do I separate myself from her so as not to endorse her behavior? Or do I risk loving her when I don't know how?

Her sins are just like mine; they're just a different brand. She and her partner have been together for years now, living in isolation from the rest of us. Underneath the layers of mess and story, her emotions are hinged like a swinging door as she looks for unwavering acceptance. Somewhere deep inside her, like the glow of a smoldering ember, remains the thought that she was made for something more than struggle. And I can deeply relate.

You see, the undeniable connection between us is that we both have struggles; it's just that mine are more socially acceptable. But sin and sickness is universal.

Sin is not just in my actions; it's a condition. It is any and all the ways I try to be my own savior. It's this wretched heart of mine. Sometimes, it's a matter of grabbing for power over people at my job, sometimes it's the lust to buy more "stuff" that will make me feel significant in front of my friends, and sometimes it's just the way I try to control my life to protect my own interests at all costs.

So, here's the connection between her and me: The bridge to reach her is repentance. If I think my sins are petty, abstract and occasional, I will have no framework to give Jesus to someone who needs Him. Indeed, we were made for more than struggle. In fact, we were made for glory. But even now, God gives purpose to our struggle, and He is in charge of all that happens to us. I don't have the power to give my friend much resolution in her life, but I can give her Jesus.

Love is not safe. Love is not efficient. I'm sure I will disappoint her as we go, and I will fail over and again in loving her well. But when you are in Jesus, your sin does not define you. Jesus' love for His sons and daughters is enough to win our hearts back from all the struggles we're bound to. And only His love can satisfy us. This is how I can love her still, without conditions. And this is the great hope I have for her heart and mine.

EVEN DEEPER
Jeremiah 2:13, John 7:38, Matthew 9:12-13, Romans 2:1; 4b; 5:8; 8:28-39, 1 Corinthians 13:1-13

PRAYER
Jesus, thank You that Your love is enough for me. I'm sorry that I mess up all the time in trying to love the people around me. May the grace You've given me motivate me to love others without condition.

❦ WHO'S THE MAN? ❦

Leslie Davies

There's a similar craving in people everywhere—namely, they want to be somebody great. Everyone wants to be The Man, to portray self-confidence and apparent control over his or her own life. We want to take credit and get the glory.

When we peer into our hearts, we see that humans have a remarkable propensity for self-glorification. Ultimately this is a defiance of God, who gives breath and life and everything to all humanity. Yet we are not only prone to this vain glorification, our society promotes it, says we have a right to it and tells us we deserve it. The media readily let us in on the lifestyles of entertainers and professional athletes who flaunt their wealth and achievements. Contestants of reality-based television shows claim it's their time to shine. Even teenage girls wear T-shirts declaring they are a "superstar" or a "hottie."

Our world could not be more mistaken.

Proverbs states that "to seek one's own glory is not glory" and provides further counsel that we need not praise ourselves, but instead, let others provide the praise.

The truth is that the glory of God is too astounding, too weighty for us to bear. We would literally die from the sight of it. A mere glimpse is what brought splendor to Moses' face, though he was hidden in the cleft of a rock.

So how do we deflect glory to the only one worthy of it? We remember that a relational God created us, and we remember that the Father, the Son and the Holy Spirit are at work, fashioning us into His likeness. We bring all of our life under the sway of His glory.

The reality of glorifying God happens when we trade in our angry words for kind ones. It happens when we suffer, when others take credit for our efforts, when we choose to believe His promises above the lies of the world. Glory happens when we let Him cultivate in us the fruit of the Spirit. Jesus spoke implicitly when He said, "By this my Father is glorified, that you bear much fruit." His shining in us will allow others to see the majesty that is beyond comprehension.

Glory doesn't happen when it's convenient for our schedules or in the way our finite minds imagine. It simply begins and ends with our Father.

So when glory happens, we'd better find a cleft in the rock ... The Man is passing by.

EVEN DEEPER
Exodus 33-34, Psalm 4, Matthew 5:13-16

PRAYER
God, forgive me for how each day, I seek to get credit for myself. Change my heart so that my desire is to point attention and praise to You. Be glorified by and pleased with my actions, words, decisions, and thoughts. You are the Glorious One.

QUANTITY TIME
Melanie Siebert

Because I was sitting nearby, I couldn't help but over-
hear. A student was talking to a friend about raising
children. "Parents today shouldn't feel so guilty for not
spending as much time with their kids," she said. "After
all, it's really about quality time, isn't it?"

My mind seized on that familiar phrase: quality time.
As the woman began discussing another topic, I thought
to myself, No. It's not just about quality time. I considered some of the typical "quality" moments between parents and children: hearing the child's first word, seeing
her first step, sharing a private joke. How can a parent
expect to be present for the first word or first step if he
only spends a few strategically allotted minutes with his
child each day? How can a parent have enough experiences in common with his child to develop private jokes
if he only plans for a minimal amount of "quality" contact in a day?

In most cases, it takes time to get to know someone,
which is why we talk about "building relationships" as if
they were edifices. Building a relationship, like building
a house, is a process requiring patience, time, and effort.
The quality of the time we spend together, it seems to
me, is dependent upon the quantity of time we spend,
and vice versa. Yet, how often do I take the "quality
time" approach to my relationship with God?

When I was a child, my family regularly attended
a traditional church. We gave God a couple hours on
Sunday mornings; the rest of the week was ours. We

lived the hours outside of church as we pleased, rarely stopping to think about God, much less to build a relationship with Him.

Later, even after I discovered the joy of personally knowing God, I largely confined my relationship with Him to specially designated "quiet times." I prayed in the mornings. The rest of the day, although I strove to live for Him, I rarely communicated with Him.

Is this a biblical approach? Jesus seemed to be in constant communication with the Father, offering up praise, praying for others, and expressing grief or confusion, sometimes spontaneously in public and sometimes alone. Paul instructed us to "pray continually" and told Timothy "night and day I constantly remember you in my prayers," indicating that prayer to him was a continual state of mind. Imagine how much richer our individual relationships with God would be if we applied this mindset to our own prayer lives.

EVEN DEEPER
Matthew 11:25; 19:13; 26:39; 27:46, John 11:41; 17, 1 Thessalonians 5:17, 2 Timothy 1:3

PRAYER
Lord, I don't want to compartmentalize my relationship with You. I want to walk with You each day and take my joys and pains to You before I take them to anyone else. Help me to hear Your voice. Thank You for Your presence.

⟊ROBBING WIDOWS⟊
Winn Collier

We have a nasty penchant for crudely drawing distinctions between sacred and secular, faith and works, redemption and justice. Themes, which naturally travel in pairs, are ripped apart, and the unfortunate result is that each loses its force.

The recipients of the prophet Malachi's brooding message, Judeans who had returned from exile to a partially restored homeland, had fallen into such a trap. Cynically content with their recent change of luck, they had adapted to a certain malaise, settling in to a rhythm where God was given a cursory nod but relegated to the corner.

God's people had abandoned their center—God, and His covenant with them. The tragic fall-out was how abandoning God led to them abandoning their unique role in the world—a "kingdom of priests" who mediated God's grace and justice to an unrighteous society.

The same is true today; when we lose our sense of God, we lose our sense of our role in the world around us. Malachi addressed this tragic abandonment by making a somewhat surprising connection. Immediately preceding the most familiar portion of Malachi—his rebuke against the people's practice of robbing God by refusing to bring the appropriate tithe to temple worship—Malachi rattles off a number of other common expressions of sin among God's people: those who oppress widows, lack love for the orphans, and refuse proper justice for immigrants. The message seems clear: There is no distinction between abandoning justice and abandoning worship; they travel in pairs. In Malachi's view, there is an inherent connection between robbing God and robbing widows.

The prophet's answer for their insincere worship was not only for them to bring in the tithe they owed, but to repent of their sinful stance toward the less fortunate.

Malachi's posture highlights an utter inconsistency—public displays or rituals of worship that have not taken root in our private life with our fellowman. We are urged not to leave our gold at the altar if we have left our neighbor hungry.

Malachi's words penetrate deep in a world bowing to the idols of consumerism, individualism, and capitalism. We construct our behemoth church campuses, insist on the latest SUV and consider it a major inconvenience if the local Super Wal-Mart isn't open twenty-four hours. And millions are starving. And HIV ravages entire nations. And children are born in a world where the "American Dream" is their highest goal.

Malachi must be heard again.

EVEN DEEPER
Malachi 3

PRAYER
God, search my heart and reveal to me the ways I've lost my sense of You by not seeing the needs of those around me. I confess that I'm often afraid or lazy. Open my eyes to the social injustices around me, and direct me in how I can help.

⚓ DEATH AND FAITH ⚓
Brett Ferguson

For most of my life, my faith was relatively stable. However, twenty months after the death of my father, my once sure faith became frighteningly insecure.

This brush with death brought discouragement and doubts like I had never experienced. In the middle of this storm of questions, I came to realize that in spite of all the teaching about faith I had ingested over the years, I knew very little.

As I've journeyed to a deeper understanding and experience of faith, it has been important for me to reclaim the biblical context in which faith grows. Faith is always expanded through difficulty. Abraham, the Father of Faith, was asked to believe and act on the idea that someone "as good as dead" could have a child. The hopes of the world were on this child, whom God promptly asked him to kill. Job was stripped of all of his wealth, the lives of his family, and his own health. Jesus looked Peter in the eye and said: "Satan has asked to sift you like wheat." And Jesus did not deny Satan that opportunity.

I have seen a bit of suffering; however, my trials do not grow my faith merely by being difficult. In the Bible, the book of James says trials grow faith by "testing" faith. I have found no greater faith-test than when God's dealings with me have led me to question my construct of the nature or existence of God.

It is here that we sense our faith, in the words of James, being "tested." Our faith is pushed to the brink, stretched beyond its capacity to survive. We feel our faith is failing, and it is. But this is good news. I am learning to embrace doubt, viewing it not as the poison of faith, but as its fertilizer.

When our faith is on the verge of disintegrating and we are helpless, we can come desperately before God. Doubt fertilizes faith by destroying faith in our beliefs and creating desperation for God Himself.

When I was told my dad was dead, I remember pounding my hands against the hot, dry Kansas ground. Twenty months later, I am still punching and kicking, crying and screaming my pain to my heavenly Father. My "faith-world" has been destroyed, yet in the middle of my doubts, my God has ample room to show me who He is. For years my faith (beliefs about God) may have impeded my relationship (knowing God). A shattered faith is a small price to pay for a deeper knowledge of my God.

EVEN DEEPER
James 1:2-18, Job 38-41

PRAYER
God, do what You have to do to draw me to You. Do what You have to do to realign my beliefs about who You are to the truth. Although I have questions, I humbly submit to whatever You have for me—good or bad.

❧ THE SAVIOR SELF ❧
Michael D. Warden

Sometimes the days become war. They blindside us
with unrelenting blows from the mundane corners of
everyday life. There is too much to do, too many fronts
to defend, too many fires to put out. There is only stress,
like a dull red blanket covering our eyes. And there
is no longer any time. There is only going. Reacting.
Surviving. Striving to save ourselves and our future. But
where does all this striving lead us? To actual victory?
Not even close. And we all know this. So what deceives
us into traveling the days as though we have strength
enough to be the savior of our own lives? Do we think
(in our omniscient wisdom) that because we cannot see
God working to make a way for us, that He must, then,
not be? Do we conclude (quietly, secretly, where even our
own thoughts can barely hear) that since God is doing
nothing, then we must somehow make a way for ourselves?

Well. I do. He is my life; I have no other. Though on
this point, I do love to pretend otherwise. And then,
having pretended for a while, just as quickly I turn and
hate the prison of defeat and isolation my pretense has
created. I am a sore excuse for a deliverer, a grace-giver, a
maker of ways. I am no good at it. The best I can man-
age against the daily onslaught is nominal survival. And
that's just on the good days. No wonder Solomon cried,
"Vanity! Vanity! All is striving after wind!" I have felt
the sting of that wind's icy breath, and I know it carries
nothing but the stench of futility. Who can hold the

wind in his hands? Better, I say, to let the wind hold you.
Carry you, in fact.

Too often, we miss Jesus. Striving the way we do always makes the distance between us and Him ache with inconsolable longing. But the damnable part of that is that it doesn't have to be so! He is there with us; He remains still. Patient. Waiting. Being God.

Of the pressures and distractions and decisions we must face each day, there is (it seems) no end. But there is only one decision that truly matters. And that is the decision to cling close to Jesus, to hang trembling to His garments, whatever battlelines form against us at our backs. Choosing not to fight in our own strength. But to believe, and to rest. There is no other option. And no other victory.

EVEN DEEPER
Psalm 27, John 16:33, Romans 8

PRAYER
Jesus, please forgive me for trying to be my own savior. I confess that I am weak. Please be my strength. I confess that I am foolish. Please be my wisdom. I confess that I don't know the way. Please make a way for me and guide me in it.

❧ MESSY BUSINESS ☙
Winn Collier

Wyatt is our fourteen-month-old, and when you piece together the etymology of his full name, he is bestowed with the gallant title of "a warrior who is famous in battle." We had no idea what we were asking for.

There are times when we would enjoy other descriptors like "docile" or "meek." Heck, there are days when we would settle for just slightly toned down mayhem.

But you don't raise a warrior by dousing his fire. We might want Wyatt to stir up a little less of a ruckus or flirt with a little less danger, but that will not yield the man we hope for him to become. Try as we might, there is no clean or pristine path to bold manhood—or to courageous womanhood. There are skinned knees and broken hearts and overzealous mishaps all along the way. It's a messy business.

This is a universal reality. As we grow older, we all find that the mess doesn't diminish. God has hopes for us, to form us into His image, to make us a people who courageously live out our created purpose in our world.

But He knows a bold faith comes only by walking many treacherous miles. So, much to our dismay, we encounter moments of terror, when we hear the dreaded news that our company is downsizing or our fiancé somehow thinks he "should move on." And we wonder if we couldn't settle for just slightly toned down mayhem.

I think Paul would commiserate well with our predicament. He had sacrificed much, given everything for The Way. I would imagine he expected some sort of a payoff, perhaps a fulfillment of his dream to see at least a mild awakening in Rome, a city holding much of his affections and aspirations.

It was not to be. Paul did return to the Empire's capital, but as a prisoner. Confined to house arrest, Paul's best days in Rome were spent writing letters. Apparently, God's hopes for Paul were for something more, something messier.

While we can be certain of the goodness of God's heart, certainty of His movements is a bit more slippery. Often times, we have no idea what we are asking for—and that is the crux of faith: trusting God with our dreams as well as our disappointments.

To abandon ourselves to God is to abandon ourselves to messiness. While this chaos is never out of His control, it is certainly out of ours. It's the same—for grown-up dreamers, as well as for little warriors.

EVEN DEEPER
Philippians 1, 2 Timothy 1:11-13, Exodus 15:2-4

PRAYER
God, I abandon myself to You, even though I know it'll be messy. I am certain that You are good. I trust You, even if things don't turn out the way I am hoping they will. Please take control.

ON SEEING GOD
Stephanie Gehring

The Bible is the story of God's ever-progressing self-revelation. God wants us to see the whole picture, or at least a bigger and bigger part of the picture. But we can only start to see once we give up believing that we have the whole truth already. To see, we must listen as though we don't have all the answers yet.

One way to see more of the picture is to pay attention to the ways in which humans outside our frame of reference see God. If you're not Catholic, pay attention to the Catholics. You may find much in their beliefs with which to disagree. But don't stop there; look deeper, and be open to the possibility that they're seeing faces of God that you miss. Could there be something important in the regular practice of confession? Could penance be a step out of guilt and toward freedom? Could the observance of holy days, of rest, of ritual and reverence be more than stodgy rules; could structure sometimes be refreshing instead of stifling?

Pay attention to churches that come from their parts of the world. What's up with Russian Orthodoxy? Not that you need to join that denomination. But what's the deal with icons? Are they really as heretical as you've always been told, or might there be more to this than you realized? Early icon painters referred to their work as "the Word of God in lines and color." Icons are said to be written, not painted, and read, or prayed with, rather than prayed to.

What is the African Church seeing that we're not?

What does the Asian Church remember that we've forgotten? What do the Jews know about God that we would do well to stay aware of? And geography is not the only direction to stretch; we need not limit ourselves to our own time, either. There are many in the past who have seen God with a clarity that made them unable to go on living their lives as before. Some of them left words that make it possible for us, too, to be changed by their visions. Some of them wrote hymns. Go to a used bookstore sometime, or to Goodwill, or to your parents' or grandparents' bookshelves, or even search online: Read the words of hymns. Whether you've ever sung them or not, whether you like singing them or not, just read the words. And listen.

It will be worth it. You'll see.

EVEN DEEPER
Colossians 3:11, Revelation 5:9-10

PRAYER
Dear Heavenly Father, reveal Yourself to me any way You want. I don't want to limit You.

WHY DO YOU DOUBT?
Winn Collier

What if you saw one who claimed to be God walking on water? What if this one who claimed to be God invited you out to test the waves? And you did … and there you stood, feet firmly planted on liquid earth. What would you do? Would an unshakable faith well up? Would questions and concerns melt away, seeming foolish now that you had seen and knew what was true? Probably not. Ask Peter.

Peter doubted. Peter wondered if Jesus was enough to handle his turmoil, perhaps if the notion of God were even true. And this was after—after—he had seen and after he had touched.

Peter was with the disciples on a small fishing vessel, tossed and rocked as the ship strained and moaned against the waves' assault. Fighting for their lives, they saw Christ walking—yes, walking—across the waves toward them. But they were unsure. Was it really Him? How could it be? Peter made what seems to be an absurd request. "If it is really You, have me come out to You."

"Come," said the figure standing on the water, in the middle of the storm.

And he did. Almost without thinking, Peter hiked up his robe, stepped over the edge of the boat, and took a few steps. On water. Peter walked on water.

But what transpires next is confusing. Peter feels the surge of the wind and sees the violence of the waves. And he doubts. Peter's faith fails, and he begins to go under. Christ pulls him up and asks him: "Why did you doubt?"

The story is unsettling. If Peter could doubt, if Peter wasn't quite sure, what does it say about my faith? If Peter wasn't certain, how can I ever be?

Peter's experience points us to an important distinction. I assume faith and certainty to be the same thing. God doesn't.

Certainty is proof. Certainty is mathematical equations and verifiable evidence. Faith, on the other hand, is holding on to God when life batters you, when all the forces of hell assault you.

Christ's question is most profound—not because Peter had seen the miraculous, but because Peter had seen Christ. Christ stood on the waves. Christ offered Peter an invitation. And He offers the same invitation to us.

There is something deeper than certainty, something deeper than proof. It is faith—faith that Christ has spoken, has breathed life into our hearts, has offered us Himself. The question is whether or not we will leap into the dark, uncertain waters of faith.

EVEN DEEPER
Matthew 14

PRAYER
Jesus, help me to hold onto You in faith. I often worry about my circumstances, but I don't want to, because I know You have my life in Your hands. More than anything, I want to follow You even if I don't have all the answers.

⅋BEAUTIFUL TIMING⅋
Monique Michel

Every day the beggar sat. He begged for change, food and probably just about anything anyone would be willing to toss his way. But no one paid him much attention. Every day someone carried him to that gate—that same exact gate. The gate was called Beautiful.

The man was anything but that. Crippled since birth, he never got to roam around and see beautiful things. He probably never wore the finest or most beautiful garments. Most likely he couldn't read, but if he could, it would have had to sting his eyes every day as he read the inscription on the gate at which he was dropped off: Beautiful. The irony of that poor old man being in front of that gate may have gone unnoticed by some, but not by the Grand Composer of the universe. For He was orchestrating something far grander than that ailing man could have ever imagined.

Every day he sat there, but today he would dance away.

He begged Peter and John that day. He wasn't specifically begging for a chance at a better life, but when you are destitute and willing to accept change, that's often what God does. So when Peter stretched out his hand to that crippled man, that man was made what he had been sitting in front of his whole life: Beautiful.

It came as a surprise to some, but that's how God does it. The crippled man skipped away, and a whole city was amazed at what two willing servants of Jesus could do. It was on that day that the crowds learned what God has been trying to teach His most stubborn, created creatures for a long while now: Everything is made Beautiful in my timing.

At one time or another, we are all like that man described in Acts 3—crippled and begging. Whether spiritually dead or perhaps just decidedly complacent, we are all looking for something or someone to make us what we are stuck right in front of—Beautiful.

Beautiful is a place at which you have to arrive yourself. No one can take you there. It's a place you have to get up off the ground to enter. It's a place where the deepest part of you reaches out and grabs for the deepest part of God. All you have to do is beg for change.

EVEN DEEPER
Acts 3, Philippians 1:6

PRAYER
I do, God—I beg for change. I have trouble seeing beauty in my life. Mostly I see disappointment and monotony. Thank You that there is beauty to be found all around me. Awake me to it!

GOD, WHAT DO YOU WANT FROM ME?

Jeremy Walden

When my wife and I were expecting our first child, I asked many questions: "Am I going to be a good father?" "How's the baby going to effect my relationship with my wife?" And I have again asked God, "What do you want from me?" and "How can I please You?"

I asked similar questions when I graduated from high school, got a new job and got married. It is also in moments of despair and confusion that we ask the big questions. I asked similar questions when my father died when I was 17.

It is in these moments that we seek direction, purpose, and clarity. One of the clearest statements about God's expectations of us is found in Micah 6:8: "But he's already made it plain how to live, what to do, what God is looking for in men and women. It's quite simple: Do what is fair and just to your neighbor, be compassionate and loyal in your love, and don't take yourself too seriously—take God seriously" (The Message).

The scene is like a cosmic courtroom. God is the plaintiff bringing a case against Judah. God's charge against them is that they have grown tired of God and have gone their own way. Judah's complaint against God is that He doesn't care about them because bad things are happening to them. God clearly points out that their suffering was due to their own sin. Then He asks them to remember all the ways He rescued and saved them. The people of Judah acknowledge their sin and seek a way to make it right with God. They suggest that they can please God if they offer more sacrifices to God. Micah screams, "No! God doesn't want more rituals. He is more interested in your behavior, your relationships with people, and in your relationship with Him."

It's easy for us to look at the people of Judah and see their hypocrisy. But how many times have we done the same thing? We realize our sin and offer to make it up to God by saying we'll go to church more, pray more, or give more. God wants us to change our life, not just a few ritualistic activities.

Micah 6:8 gives simple guidance. God's expectations sound simple enough—to do right, to love people, and to have a close relationship with Him. Yet even when God's expectations are in their simplest form, we realize that we cannot meet His requirements. Thus, we must do like many others before us: seek His grace.

EVEN DEEPER
Micah

PRAYER
Father, thank You for making it clear what You want from me, but I confess that I cannot be fair, compassionate, loyal, or devoted to You by my own strength. Move me with grace and power from Your Spirit.

❦ MOTIVES OF DISCIPLESHIP ❧
Will Walker

Means and ends. Motives and outcomes. Habits and desires. These are the issues of discipleship.

Your faith in Christ has in some way compelled you to do things you probably wouldn't do otherwise: Go to church, read the Bible, confess your faults, sing out loud around other people, etc. Such things often become indicators. When we see people raise their hands during worship or lead a small group, we tend to assume something about their spiritual maturity, and likewise when we see someone sin.

Mark illustrates this in a subtle contrast of Peter's mother-in-law (1:29-31) and a leper (1:40-45). The outcomes are the same: Jesus heals both of them. The contrast is in their motives, which is evidenced by their response. When Jesus "came to her (Peter's mother-in-law) and raised her up, taking her by the hand, the fever left her, and she waited on them." What she hoped to gain by being healed was the opportunity to serve Jesus. The leper, on the other hand, takes a different course. Jesus gave him specific instruction to "see to it that you say nothing to anyone … but he went out and began to proclaim it freely and to spread the news around." His response reveals that what he really wanted from Jesus was the opportunity to get on with his life.

If you have a terminal illness and someone heals you, you at least make sure to do the one thing he asks of you, right? Well, you do if the opportunity to follow and obey Him is what you wanted in the first place. But if our motivation in asking God for healing or help is really just a plea for a quick fix for our discomfort so we can get back to our normal life, then perhaps that is why sin can be so easy at times. And perhaps that is also why we pray less when "things are going good."

Sometimes I don't feel like reading the Bible, or praying, or serving, or singing. I am too often ruled by the urgent and drawn to comfort and ease. My complaining and whining is the evidence. But these moods and tendencies are not insurmountable. Jesus is able to transform them at the deepest levels of our desires if that is actually what we want. And if it is, then we can force ourselves into disciplines and habits even when we don't feel like it, and they will become our delight so long as our aim is nothing less than that Christ be formed in us.

EVEN DEEPER
Colossians 1, Luke 14: 25-34

PRAYER
Lord, I'm sorry that so often, I'm just looking for a quick fix from You. Make me a disciple whose honest desire is to serve and follow You.

ℰSCRATCHING GOD'S BACK?℧
Garry Geer

We make a mistake when we think serving God is equivalent to serving men. When we serve our neighbor, our friend, our spouse, or our coworker, we subconsciously create a system of payment and debt. We build up "favors" with one another. Since I have scratched your back, both of us understand that one day you will scratch mine. Of course, this is never spoken out loud, and we would fiercely deny such expectations. But it's part of our ingrained human condition. God doesn't play by those rules.

Several weeks ago I was in prayer, asking God to give me strength and grace to get through some various "crises" that had entered my life. It was a fine prayer, with lots of adjectives and long, drawn-out, rambling phrases. Underneath it all was the expectation that since I had done plenty for God, He owed me help. I had scratched His back. It was time for God to offer a little scratch in return.

Truth surfaced in my heart: "God doesn't need my service. He wants it, but He doesn't need it." I didn't like this line of thinking, so I ignored it for a bit—but it bullied its way back in. "God doesn't need me."

If God didn't need my service, then my failures didn't hamper His will from being accomplished. My victories don't provide spiritual "leverage" to convince God to listen to my prayer.

This revelation forces the question, "Why should I serve God, if my service isn't necessary?" There is the whole obedience factor, but I do think it goes deeper.

While I mow our lawn, my five-year-old boy often likes to stand in front of me and grip the mower handle as I push. I don't need him to mow my lawn. It will be accomplished whether he tags along or not. But he wants to be with me. He wants to do what his father is doing. He wants to be in on accomplishing the tasks his father believes are important. His service is a precious and vital form of fellowship with me.

Is there any difference with our Father? He supplies us with the opportunity, the desire and the ability to accomplish His will. He guides our fumbling hands, removes the true burden from our shoulders, and sees that we do not hurt ourselves. In our audacity, we return to Him, claiming that we deserve special favor for our "service." Let it be enough for us to say that we were able to spend time with our Father.

EVEN DEEPER
Luke 17

PRAYER
Father, forgive me for thinking You need my help. Change my attitude so that my acts of service will be truly selfless—not hoping I'll get something in return, but just enjoying working alongside You. Thank You for the opportunity.

HIGHER PLACES
Karen Francis

For some reason, despite my increasingly selective memory, I can remember every single moment in my life when I have stood on top of a mountain or a hill. I cannot always remember the view, or exact location or year, but I always remember the feeling and the company. It would seem now in retrospect that these occasions rarely occur with people you do not like or do not know well.

Perhaps we connect with these people on a deeper level once we arrive at our destination. Perhaps we only attempt such expeditions with people we can stand to be with for a length of time. Or perhaps, without prior knowledge, we somehow could see that by spending this time in nature, and by surveying such an exhilarating view, we would seal that memory forever and make those persons with us a part of our life experience.

I've never climbed Mount Sinai, but a friend of mine has. As she related her experience of the heat, camel ride, and limited water supplies, I felt insignificant. One intuitively knows that a landscape so rugged and with such a history would certainly leave you in awe of creation.

God spoke to Moses out of that mountain, albeit through billowing smoke, fire, and earthquakes. When Moses returned from his expedition, his face shined so bright he was forced to wear a veil to cover the after effects of witnessing the glory and presence of God. In Scripture, this mountain grows in its legend as the place where God showed up.

Just as God spoke out of the mountain at Sinai, I

believe He still speaks to those who venture into nature and at times, the wilderness. Whether alone or with friends, few can deny that when they stand on top of a mountain they are overwhelmed with the question, "Who is there like you?"

There are numerous such places and numerous such moments. Whether volcanoes, earthquakes, huge mountain ranges, or the glaciers and geysers of Iceland, all these are magnificent displays of His might and strength.

So when you next make arrangements to go walking or climbing with that friend you can't wait to spend time with, do not be surprised when your conversations at the summit go deeper and you feel your mind broadening. It's God's way of speaking. Make room to hear from Him.

EVEN DEEPER
Deuteronomy 4, Exodus 19 and 24, Psalm 65

PRAYER
God, reveal Your bigness to me—in forests, mountains, lakes, prairie fields. Reveal to me my own smallness. Speak. Give me the ability to hear You and understand You.

✑DRY AND TIRED✑
Chris Aytes

No matter who we are, or how long we've pursued a relationship with God, everyone goes through what we've come to call "desert experiences." These are hard times with God, which always seem to offer some great revelation or lesson in the end. Many call these times the most poignant way God speaks to them in their life. But does God really intend on us going through those times? Is that really part of the plan?

We call these desert experiences as a biblical allusion to Moses and the nation of Israel. But if we read through Genesis again, we may find that they were left in the desert largely in part to continued rebellion and disobedience.

What does this say about our own spiritual journeys?

When we get to a place where we don't feel God's love, it is quite possible we've not been around God enough to let Him love on us.

God doesn't stop loving us when we stray from consistent, meaningful fellowship with Him, or when we don't live up to our calling, as Paul wrote about in Ephesians 4. In fact, God waits patiently.

We must realize that life isn't some science experiment. God created us because He wanted love from someone who had a choice to love Him or not. Jesus pointed out that the most important things to do in life is to love God and love people.

The idea of God being disappointed in us when we do stray is not what the "new covenant" is about. The law does still exist, and we are called to honor it with our lives. However, God is not foiled by our failures. As Hebrews says, He disciplines us as His children out of love for us and a desire to make us righteous.

Righteousness is hard. While righteous living is of utmost importance, God is still all about friendship. Jeremiah 31:2-3 says, "This is what the LORD says: 'The people who survive the sword will find favor in the desert; I will come to give rest to Israel.' The LORD appeared to us in the past, saying: 'I have loved you with an everlasting love; I have drawn you with loving-kindness.'" And like Romans 2:4 tells us, "God's kindness leads you toward repentance."

So when you start thinking you haven't been reading your Bible like you're "supposed to," or praying like "you should be," ask yourself if it's a lack of biblical knowledge and/or token prayers that's making you feel dry and tired, or if it's maybe caused by not spending time hanging out with the only one who can give us real rest.

EVEN DEEPER
Matthew 11, Psalm 62

PRAYER
Father, I'm burnt out from attempting to be righteous by trying harder. I want to rest in You. I want to understand how You draw me with kindness. Help me to live out of the love You shower on me.

❦ SHUDDERING IN SILENCE ❧
Doug Floyd

Elijah is running for his life. He runs to the very edge of the kingdom of Judah, and then continues into the wilderness until he can run no more. Falling beneath a Juniper tree, Elijah cries out to die. He yields his spirit up to God, and everything goes dark.

But he doesn't die. An angel wakes him, feeds him, and sends him deeper into the desert.

This same Elijah proclaimed the rain would stop in Israel and it did, raised a dead boy to life, humiliated and killed prophets of Baal. This prophet of God who came from nowhere must now find God in no place—Mt. Horeb.

Mt. Horeb, also known as Mt. Sinai, is the same place Moses met God. Cloaked in lightening and smoke, Moses entered into the terrifying grip of God's grace. The children of Israel could not touch this mountain for fear of mortal danger.

In this holy, mysterious place, Elijah ascends to find God. He leaves behind human civilization, human strength, and human wisdom. In the hole of a cave, he waits for an audience with the Creator.

Suddenly a violent wind rips through the mountain. The intensity is so great that the mountain begins to crumble and shake. There is an explosion. Fire surrounds Elijah like lava consuming the land. And then everything stops. Shuddering silence. God is present.

Elijah has come to the end of himself. He must face his images, his idols, and his limitations of God. He must face the fact that he is finite and fallen. His limited view of God and his inflated view of self fall before the holy quiet of the Creator.

We need the desert. We need our own revelations challenged—again and again. Like Elijah, we think we understand God. He knew Him in outward power; he faced Him in living silence. In our understanding, we seek to domesticate the untamed Creator. Then like a genie in a bottle, we wait for Him to appear and grant us our wishes.

Like Elijah, we compare ourselves with others. From our own deeply flawed perception, we determine some are better than us and some are worse. We often secretly despise those around us who succeed. But then we are humiliated in His holiness and face our absolute dependence upon His mercy and grace. We breathe every breath by the grace of God. Lord, have mercy! We go to the desert to be stripped naked. For when we are naked before the Lord, He can clothe us with His glory.

EVEN DEEPER
1 Kings 17-19

PRAYER
Lord, forgive me of my pride. Forgive me for thinking I've got You all figured out. You are the Holy One, the Merciful One, the Gracious One. Thank You that You cover me with Your holiness, mercy, and grace.

❦ FAITH LIKE A CHILD ❧
Brandon Smith

A passage of Scripture that has defined Jesus in a lot of ways and long made people think about what it means to be a Christ-follower is Matthew 18:1-4: "At that time the disciples came to Jesus and asked, 'Who is the greatest in the kingdom of heaven?' He called a little child and had him stand among them. And he said: 'I tell you the truth, unless you change and become like little children, you will never enter the kingdom of heaven. Therefore, whoever humbles himself like this child is the greatest in the kingdom of heaven.'"

But what does Jesus desire from our lives when He asks us to become like little children? In a time when children were disregarded by the wise men of the society, Jesus turned the tables and told us that unless we shift the course of our lives and grow to be like children, He wants no part of us.

My daughter, in all her wisdom as an infant, has taught me more about this startling truth than any preacher doing his thing on Sunday morning. When life becomes too much for her to handle, Eden cries. She yells out for help. Although she can't choose words to express her frustration, discomfort or anger, she knows when she raises her voice, she is answered.

Where, in the course of growing up, do we lose this sense of dependence? When does it suddenly become okay to try to handle life on our own? We, as Christ-followers, must remember that we don't have to live by our own might. Life is hard. The words of King David must become ours: "In my distress I called to the Lord; I cried to my God for help" (Psalm 18:6).

Jesus' teachings regarding little children were revolutionary in the time and culture in which he walked the land. But Jesus was merely revealing to us the truth about ourselves. He understood that we have grown up too fast. We have sacrificed a child-like faith for "maturity."

Eden, in her nine months of life, has taught me the beauty of being a child. She has reminded me of Jesus' desire for children of the King to cry out to our Father, to climb into His open arms and to embrace innocence in a scary world.

EVEN DEEPER
Matthew 19:13-14, Psalm 18

PRAYER
Father, I'm so stubborn. I'm always trying to fix my own problems and be self-sufficient, but I just make things worse. Come in and be my daddy, hold me, and carry my worries. You are bigger.

❧ NO CONCEPT OF HOLINESS ❧
Daniel Parkins

The sun was shining on my lap as the car "raced" down the street going almost twenty-two miles per hour. My "Meme" was driving, a wonderfully older woman with soft features and an even softer touch, but I couldn't help but shade my face in embarrassment as the other cars flew by. Within fifteen minutes, four people had honked at us and had given unmentionable crude gestures. My impatience was actualized as I challenged Meme to drive "just a little faster …"

I believe our culture has lost its concept of the holiness of God, and this stems from our loss of respect for those whom are older. Think about it—when was the last time you were driving, saw that a senior was the cause of the traffic you had been behind, and smiled in veneration? No, if you are anything like me, you say something more along the lines of, "Figures," rather than smile.

In order to truly grasp an idea, we tend to compare it to something familiar—something we can hold on to. With the idea of holiness, that something is respect, stemming from our interactions with those who have "earned it." But as someone in our present culture, I have been bred to believe that "older" people no longer lend a helping hand in life, but are seen as a hindrance, especially when driving a car.

When respect is understood in the growing connotation of the postmodern culture that has engulfed our generation, it can only be seen as relative. It must be earned precisely the way each individual defines it.

Respect isn't derived from title or position; nor is it derived from history or actions. Respect is up to the individual who sees himself or herself as having the power to dictate and appropriate that respect. And so we have this concept of God where He too needs to "earn" our respect.

We must reclaim the holiness of God; we must begin to swim in the unfathomable waters of the most Holy God. We view ourselves much higher than we should. We so often judge God's action against what we want, and if the two wills do not line up together, our respect and concept of holiness is tainted. We need to stop yelling at God who is driving our lives, "Just a little faster," and start smiling in trust and understanding. God is in control, and He is a Holy God indeed.

EVEN DEEPER
Isaiah 66:1-2, Isaiah 40:30-31, Jeremiah 9:23-24

PRAYER
Lord, humble me and reveal to me how mind-bendingly holy You are. Give me a right understanding of respect and holiness.

ᴓ FORMED, BUT ALWAYS BEING FORMED ᴓ

Scott J. Pearson

Child psychologists refer to the various stages of
human formation as infant, toddler, pre-pubescent, ado-
lescent and young adult. After graduation from college,
unless something significant happens, our formation is
considered to be, for the most part, complete. That is,
our values have become relatively concretized, still mold-
able, but entrenched enough that they are difficult to
change. All that seems to be left is to pour ourselves into
a career, considering all the major character formation to
be completed.

Christian development often works similarly. Many
people accept Christ in their younger years, often with
much elation. Then over time, the enthusiasm retreats
as the reality of responsible adult life sets in. The aim
of Christian living often becomes a balance between
answering life's demands and not losing Christ in the
hubbub of daily life.

The world surrounds us with objects and information,
and we unfortunately become like the things on which
we focus. The challenge is to remember that our hearts
are hidden with Christ in God. A couple ways to attempt
this are the repetition of prayers ("God be glorified," or
"Jesus, have mercy on me a sinner") and constant dialog
with God about the joys and frustrations of life, however
trivial they may be. This keeps our minds on the invisible in the midst of the visible.

Part of the hope Christianity offers is that we are never
completely formed. While life shapes much of who we

are, God does the forming, pointing us to the template of Christ. And this crafting is always in progress.

And this entopic growth provides hope. We are never fully there; in Christ's light, we are always growing, even in the most mundane of circumstances. When the newness of life, of careers, and of other responsibilities wears off, the light of Christ draws us onward.

Even as we complete the most boring of tasks, Christ—not our efforts but Christ's—is renewing us, restoring us. Even as we sinfully rebel, Christ's hand is there, so the Scriptures promise, holding us fast.

Formation is a delightfully hopeful process, because each day's progress is a wonder. Each moment can be seen in the light of Christ. Each event guided by the hand of the Creator and Sustainer is providentially making us like Christ, fashioning us in His image and transforming us in His character.

So, we can rest assured—God is always at work on our behalf. And we can embrace humility—we are always in need of guidance and grace.

EVEN DEEPER
Colossians 3, 2 Corinthians 4, Psalm 139

PRAYER
Thank You, Lord, that You are continually making me more like You. Renew me and restore me this very day. As I drive, as I work, as I eat, form me into Your likeness.

AUTHOR INDEX

A Begging Faith
Andrew Albers is a graduate student at MIT where he is doing research to figure out how to save the world.

Dry And Tired
Chris Aytes is a writer, singer/songwriter, and co-youth director with his wife, Renelle, for the First United Methodist Church, in Great Bend, Kansas.

Drawing From the Well
Kate Bryan is a twenty-four-year-old art and writing student living in Portland, Oregon.

A Backwards World, Living In Advent, Messy Business, Robbing Widows, Subversive Transformation, The Risk of Hope, Welcome To The Banquet, Why Do You Doubt?
Winn Collier is a writer and a pastor of a university church, Downtown Community Fellowship, in Clemson, South Carolina.

Extravagent Reality, Who's The Man?
Leslie Davies is a freelance writer and co-director of Halo Hoops (*www.halohoops.com*). She resides in central Oregon with her husband, Dave, and their two-year-old son, Skyler.

Death And Faith
Brett Ferguson and his wife Rachel live in Denver, Colorado, where Brett serves as a pastor to emerging generations and single adults at Riverside Church.

Perfect World, Shuddering In Silence
Doug Floyd directs a retreat ministry, works in advertising, and pastors a liturgical house church.

Eternity—Right Under Your Nose, The Life And Death Of An Expectation
Allison Foley spends her time working at Starbucks and volunteering with InterVarsity Christian Fellowship at Boston College.

Higher Places
Karen Francis is from picturesque Northern Ireland, and now lives in bonny Scotland where she works with Salmon growers and loves to write.

Scratching God's Back?
Garry Geer lives on the back roads of west central Indiana with his wife and assorted children.

Better Than A Fairytale, Holding Light, Hope Remains, Looking Up, On Seeing God, The Voice Of Expectation
Stephanie Gehring is a twenty-two-year-old self-employed portrait artist, high school math tutor and freelance writer. She spent the first sixteen years of her life in Germany and now lives in Portland, Oregon.

Hope Now
Eric Hurtgen is an artist, musician, writer, and teacher who lives with his wife, Amanda, in Charlotte, North Carolina.

From Reflection to Reality
Erika Larson is a writer and editor in Orlando, Florida. She likes romantic things.

Beautiful Timing
Monique Michel is a twenty-one-year-old college senior majoring in mass communications. She wishes that she knew what God expects her to do with that degree.

No Concept of Holiness
Daniel Parkins is the Emerging Generations Director at Southwest Community Church.

Formed, But Always Being Formed
Scott J. Pearson is a computer programmer for the Arizona Genomics Computational Laboratory in Tucson, Arizona.

Wait, Hope, Trust
Tara Ringham works in prayer ministry and inner city children's ministry at the Wesley Foundation at the University of Georgia.

Quantity Time
Melanie Seibert works as a copywriter for a catalog
and Internet retailer in Charlottesville, Virginia.

Faith Like a Child
Brandon Smith lives in Kearney, Nebraska, where he
works as a campus minister on a university campus.
His daughter, Eden, is expecting her first little brother
or sister in September.

God, What Do You Want From Me?
Jeremy Walden is a husband, father, former youth
minister, owner of Next Gen Publishing, co-author
of *Dating Q&A*, and a fan of reality TV shows.

Motives Of Discipleship
Will Walker works for Campus Crusade for Christ
and makes his home in Austin, Texas, with his wife
Debbie, two-year-old son Ethan, and skittish mutt
Abby.

The Savior Self
Michael D. Warden is a full-time author and life
coach living in Austin, Texas. Learn more about his
life and work at *www.michaelwarden.com*.

The Struggle To Love
Derek Webb released his solo debut, *She Must And
Shall Go Free* (INO), after ten years as a member of
the folk-rock group Caedmon's Call.

ALSO AVAILABLE IN THIS SERIES:

Deeper Walk, Vol. 1: God of the Desert and God of Greatness
Deeper Walk, Vol. 2: God of Mercy and God of Relationship
Available online at www.RELEVANTstore.com

For more devotionals like these, check out the Deeper Walk section
in each issue of RELEVANT magazine, a publication reaching spiritually
passionate, culturally savvy twentysomethings.
www.RELEVANTmagazine.com